Apples

By Julie Haydon

Contents

The Apple Orchard

Yesterday, Mum and I went to an apple orchard to buy some apples.

We walked between rows of apple trees. There were lots of apples on the trees.

Workers were picking the red, shiny apples.
They had big bags over their shoulders.
They climbed ladders to reach the apples,
and put them in the bags.

When their bags were full,
the workers tipped the apples
into big boxes at the end
of the rows of trees.

Then a tractor took the boxes
to a big shed,
called the packing house.

Mum and I went inside the packing house.
We saw the apples being washed
and sorted.

The apples that were good enough to sell
were packed into bags and boxes.

Big trucks took these apples
from the packing house
to shops and markets
for people to buy.

Most of the apples were taken to factories to be made into drinks and foods.

The rest of the apples were sold at the orchard.
Mum and I bought some apples.
I ate one and it tasted delicious.

I learnt a lot about apple orchards yesterday.

The Apple Juice Test

Goal

To test if apple juice tastes best when it is mixed with carrot juice or when it is mixed with grape juice.

Materials

You will need:

- a juicer
- 2 glasses
- a chopping board
- a knife
- 4 apples
- 1 carrot
- 1 bunch of red grapes
- an adult to help.

Steps

1. Wash the apples, carrot and grapes.

2. Ask an adult to cut the apples and carrot into large pieces.

Apple and Carrot Juice

3. Put a glass under the juicer's spout.

4. Put two apples and one carrot into the juicer. Turn the juicer on, with the help of an adult.

5. Wait until the juice flows into the glass.

6. Turn the juicer off.

7. Clean the juicer.

Apple and Grape Juice

8. Put a clean glass under the juicer's spout.

9. Put two apples and the red grapes into the juicer. Turn the juicer on, with the help of an adult.

10. Wait until the juice flows into the glass.

11. Turn the juicer off.

12. Clean the juicer.

13. Taste the apple and carrot juice.

14. Taste the apple and grape juice.

15. Decide which juice you like best.